The Boy Who Couldn't Fly

WALKER PEACOCK, PSY.D.

ISBN 979-8-89345-836-7 (paperback)
ISBN 979-8-89345-837-4 (digital)

Copyright © 2024 by Walker Peacock, Psy.D.

All rights reserved. No part of this publication may be reproduced, distributed, or transmitted in any form or by any means, including photocopying, recording, or other electronic or mechanical methods without the prior written permission of the publisher. For permission requests, solicit the publisher via the address below.

Christian Faith Publishing
832 Park Avenue
Meadville, PA 16335
www.christianfaithpublishing.com

Printed in the United States of America

This book is dedicated to my first and greatest owl, Sara Beth Peacock.

1

Once upon a time, there was a prince who lived in a castle. He was a young prince and the only heir to the throne, so his parents—the king and the queen—were quite protective over him.

The king and queen would not allow the boy to leave the castle walls until he reached the age of ten. But they brought teachers and children into the kingdom every day so that the boy could learn and play.

When the boy wasn't in school or playing with friends, he liked to sit by his window and look out at the woods surrounding the castle. He had never seen any animals (not even a mouse because the queen liked her castle to be very clean), but he loved listening to the beautiful and exciting noises coming from the woods. He desperately wanted to experience it for himself.

2

The night before his tenth birthday, the boy was so excited that he could barely sleep. As soon as the sun peeked over the distant hills, the boy sprang from bed and got dressed as quickly as he could.

The king and queen still felt a bit worried, but they were calmed by the look of excitement on their son's face. They got dressed, had some breakfast, and escorted their son to the woods.

When they reached the edge of the woods, the king and queen knelt down to kiss and hug their son before his big journey. The king took a whistle from inside his pocket and handed it to his son. "Use this if you get lost or if you feel scared. We will come to you immediately."

The boy took the whistle and promised that he would use it if he was in trouble. He turned back to wave to his parents before he dashed into the woods.

3

The boy was amazed at the sights and sounds that surrounded him once he was in the woods. He marveled at the timid mice, the scurrying squirrels, and the enormous elephants.

But the boy stopped in his tracks, speechless, when he saw a mockingbird fly overhead and land gently on a nearby tree branch. The boy had never seen a bird before, and the bird had never seen a boy before.

"How does it *do* that?" the boy wondered to himself.

"Do what?" the mockingbird asked.

"Move through the air," the boy responded before he realized that he was *talking to an animal!*

"Oh, you must mean flying. It's easy. Watch." And the mockingbird flapped its wings, lifted off the branch, and flew a large circle before landing back on the branch.

4

The boy clapped his hands and laughed and said, "I want to do that!"

The mockingbird said, "Like I said, it's easy. Just flap your wings."

So the boy flapped his arms, like the mockingbird had showed him, but nothing happened.

The mockingbird said, "You're not flapping hard enough."

So the boy flapped his arms like crazy, but still nothing happened.

The mockingbird said, "Tsk. If you really cared, you'd be able to fly," and it flew away.

5

The boy was confused. He *really did* want to fly. He *really had* tried. He did exactly what Mockingbird told him to do. But Mockingbird, having wings, was clearly more of an expert on flying than the boy was. And the mockingbird said that the boy doesn't care. So the boy became angry with himself for not caring, and he sat down to have a good cry.

Before long, the boy remembered that he had come to the forest to *see* things and not to *cry*. So he dusted himself off, wiped his eyes, and was ready to continue his journey, when a crow landed on a nearby branch.

The crow said, "Why are you crying?"

The boy said, "Because I want to fly, but the mockingbird said that I don't care enough."

The crow said, "Hmmph. Well, mockingbirds aren't as smart as us, crows. All you have to do is flap your wings."

The boy said, "I tried that, but it doesn't work. See?" And he flapped his arms as hard as he could.

6

The crow looked for a moment and said, "Mm hmm. I see the problem. You need to jump as you flap your wings, and then you'll already be in the air."

So the boy jumped as high as he could while flapping his arms as hard as he could, but he kept landing on his feet.

The boy tried again and again but still wasn't able to fly. The crow gave the boy a disappointed look and said, "Tsk. You're just not trying hard enough. If you weren't so lazy, you'd be able to fly." And the crow flew away.

7

He was exhausted after jumping and flapping, and he thought that he had tried *really, really hard*. But Crow had just told him that he was lazy, and Crow was another expert on flying. So the boy became angrier with himself and began to cry even harder than before.

But the boy still had much exploring to do. So once again, he got up and dusted himself off and continued his walk through the woods. A short while later, the boy saw a mighty eagle. It was beautiful and looked quite regal. *This looks like a very important bird*, the boy thought to himself. *He'll be able to help me for sure.*

8

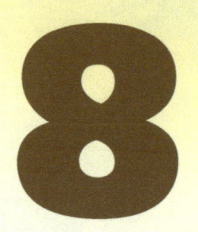

The eagle looked down at the boy and said, "You must be the boy that crow and mockingbird told me about. They told me that you were headed this way, and they warned me that you're a lazy boy who says that he *wants* to fly but doesn't seem to really care.

"But that is no matter. For I am Eagle, the biggest and strongest bird in these woods. And if I can't teach you to fly, nobody can. Let's see what you've learned so far."

So the boy jumped as high as he could jump and flapped his arms as hard as he could flap. He kept jumping and flapping as long as he could because he really was a hard worker, and he *really, really* cared. All the while, Eagle looked down at him, watching intensely.

9

Eventually, Eagle spread his giant wings and motioned for the boy to stop. "I see what the problem is," he said. "You're just standing, jumping, and flapping. You need to take a running start."

The boy was feeling very tired at this point, but he didn't want Eagle to think he was lazy. So he mustered up all the energy he could, ran as fast as he could, flapped his arms harder than he had ever flapped them, and jumped higher than he had ever jumped before.

10

Crash! The boy fell to the ground, skinning his knee. He felt the tears well up in his eyes, but he fought them back because he didn't want to seem weak. Eagle flew from his perch and landed on the ground in front of where the boy sat.

"Well, it's like I said, boy," the eagle said with disappointment. "I'm the best flying teacher in these woods. But how can I teach you if you're not going to listen or pay attention?" And Eagle flew away.

11

At this point, the boy couldn't hold his tears back any longer. If the mighty eagle, the best flying teacher in the woods, couldn't teach him, then he must really be *lazy*. He must really *not care*. He *just didn't listen*.

The boy cried very hard for a very long time, and when he looked up again, he noticed that it was getting dark. The boy began to feel scared. He took the whistle out of his pocket and was about to blow into it. But just then, he heard a giant ruffle of wings above him. The boy looked up to see a large owl, almost as big as the boy, looking quizzically down at him.

12

After a moment, the owl asked, "Why are you crying?"

And the boy said, "Because I want to fly, but I can't. Mockingbird said it's because I don't care. Crow said it's because I'm lazy. And Eagle said it's because I don't pay attention."

Owl chuckled gently and said, "That's ridiculous. Of course, you can't fly. You're a boy."

The boy sniffled and looked up at the owl. "I…I can't fly?" he asked.

The owl smiled warmly and said, "Hold out your arms like this." And with this, the owl spread his wings as far as he could. After the boy had done the same, the owl asked him, "Now what's different between you and me?"

The boy looked at the owl and then at himself and said, "My arms are skinny, and yours are big and soft."

The owl said, "That's right. I have wings and feathers. You have arms and hands. No matter how much you care, how hard you work, or how much you pay attention, you're not made to fly."

13

The boy looked at his skinny, featherless arms a little longer and then let them fall to his side with a thump. "Oh, okay. T-thank you, sir," he said. And with that, he began to walk sadly away.

"Wait a minute, boy," the owl called after him. "Why are you walking away?"

"Because I'm a boy. I don't have wings, and so I cannot fly," the boy replied. "Thank you so much for helping me, sir, but I have to go home."

14

The owl said, "Just one more moment, boy. Perhaps the problem isn't with you but with those who have tried to teach you. Mockingbird didn't care enough to teach you the right way. Crow was too lazy to teach you the right way, and Eagle wasn't paying attention to his student. Well, I'm paying attention, and I see something very important."

"What's that?" the boy asked.

"Well," the owl replied, "what do you have instead of wings and feathers?"

The boy stopped, puzzled, and said, "Hair. I have hair."

"Yes," said the owl. "And what else do you have?"

"A nose? Toes? A belly button? Freckles?" the boy asked.

15

"Yes, yes, yes, and yes," said the owl patiently as he began to gently wave the tips of his wings. "And what else?"

The boy saw the owl gently fanning the feathers at the ends of his wings. The owl looked at his wing tips and then back at the boy and then back to the wingtips, with the hint of a smile on his beak.

So the boy spread his own arms out, like the owl, and waved his own wing tips—err, fingertips—and then it struck him. "Fingers! I have fingers!"

"Excellent," said the owl. "And what can you do with fingers?"

"Well…," started the boy, somewhat confused, "I can eat with them. I can comb my hair. I can throw rocks. I can scratch my back. I can tie my shoes. I can clean my ears. I can build with blocks."

16

"That's it!" hooted the owl with excitement.

"What's *it*?" asked the boy. "Cleaning my ears?"

"No, young man," the owl replied, "if you can build, you can build what you do not have. Come back to this spot tomorrow, and I will teach you."

The boy ran home with a smile on his face and joy in his heart. He told his parents all about his exciting day and promised to do *all* of his chores first thing in the morning if they would let him return to the forest to learn from the owl.

17

The boy returned to the forest each day after his lessons and chores. He cared. He worked hard. He listened. He learned. And he flew.

18

The end.

About the Author

Walker Peacock is a clinical psychologist in Houston, where he lives with his wife and daughter. Growing up with undiagnosed ADHD, Dr. Peacock often heard from coaches and teachers that he was stupid or lazy or that he just didn't care. If it weren't for his parents and a collection of very special teachers and therapists, he may have just started to believe it.

If there is one attribute that made this latter group of mentors so special, it would be their curiosity. Rather than teach every child the same way, they instead worked to understand how each child learned, and then encouraged the child to lean into it, to let their strengths compensate for their weaker areas.

In his professional practice, Dr. Peacock works with adolescents and adults whose emotional and/or learning disorders cause them to question their own strengths and abilities. This book is inspired by their incredible journeys and is written not just for them but also for their parents, coaches, and teachers.